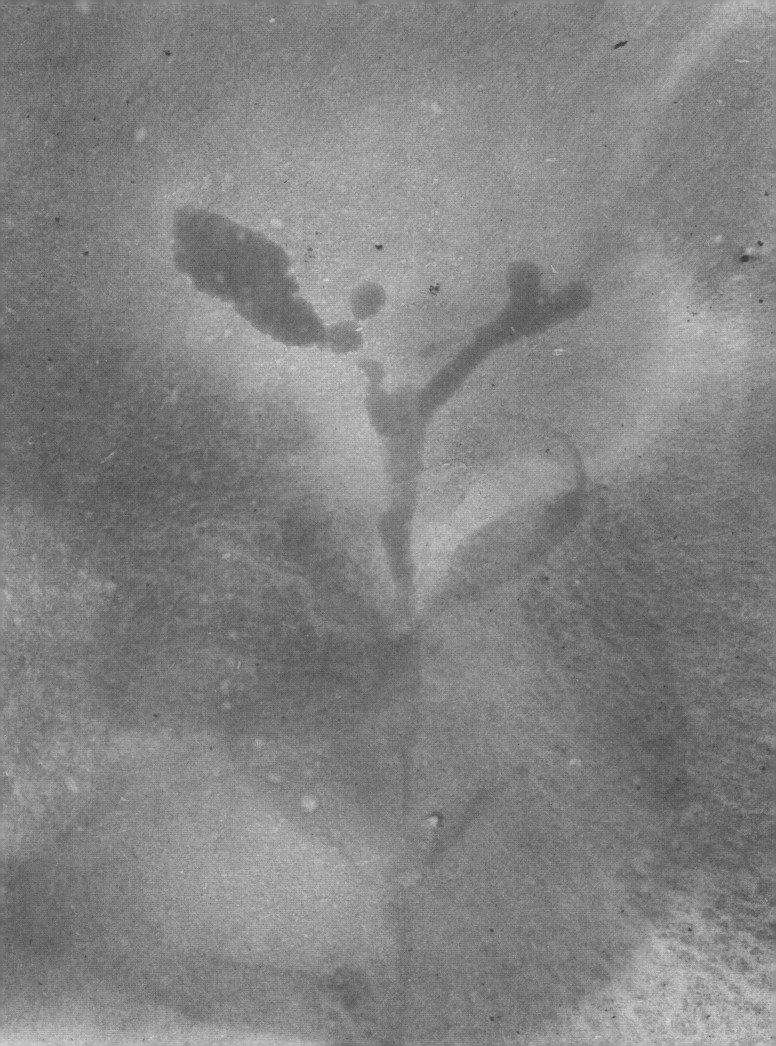

A Seed Takes Root

a True Story

Michele Oka Doner

tra.publishing

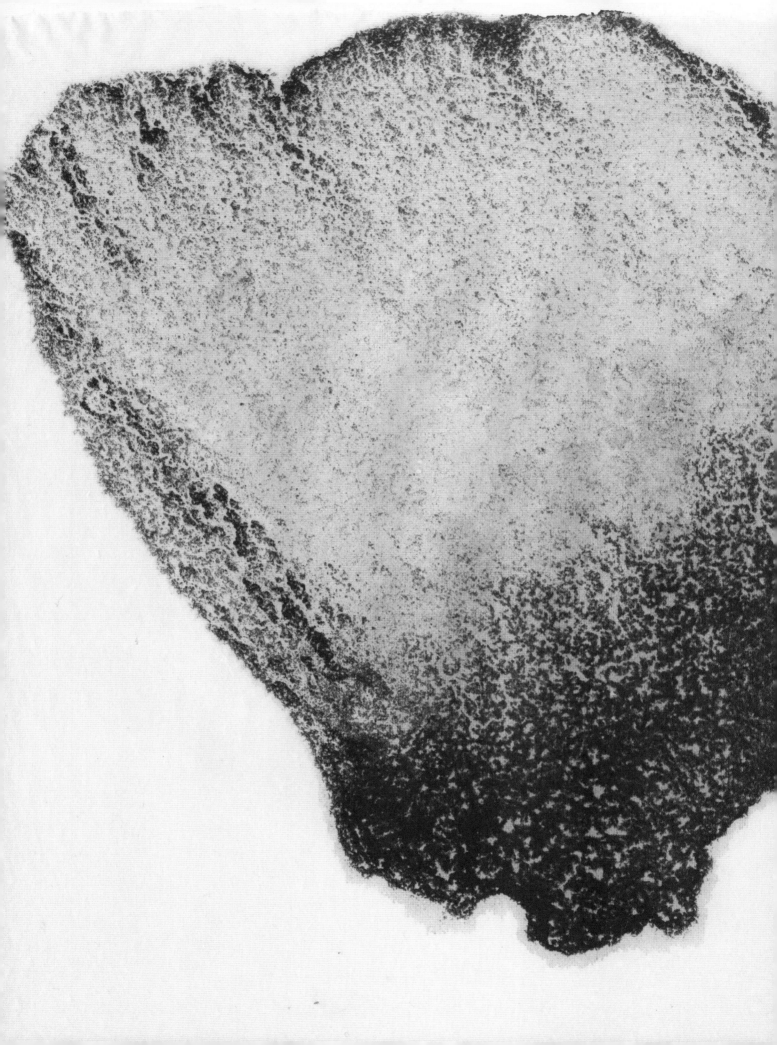

Almost 75 years have passed since the story I am about to tell you took place. It is a true story yet it appears dim and faint in a changing world. as the shadows are gathering around me and my eyesight fades I share the story of the <u>Banyan Tree</u> and its <u>mysteries</u>

at the rising of the sun each day a small girl woke up in a house in Miami Beach. It was a time of peace that followed two great wars. The girl heard adults speak of this sadness but they would quiet their voices when they knew she was listening. The sun shined, food was plentiful, and there were many books to read in the house. She carried them to her room, spread them out on the floor, and looked for answers to things she wanted to understand

She was a curious girl

The house was pink
It sat on the corner of
Fairgreen Drive,
a crooked street one block
long

It was called Fairgreen because the street was surrounded with the foliage of flowers and many trees, tall palms with large fronds and mango trees that never failed to bloom seasonally

The mango flowers went
from bud to blossom
then fruited quickly,
seeds of the earth that
swelled and burst forth
in the tropical heat

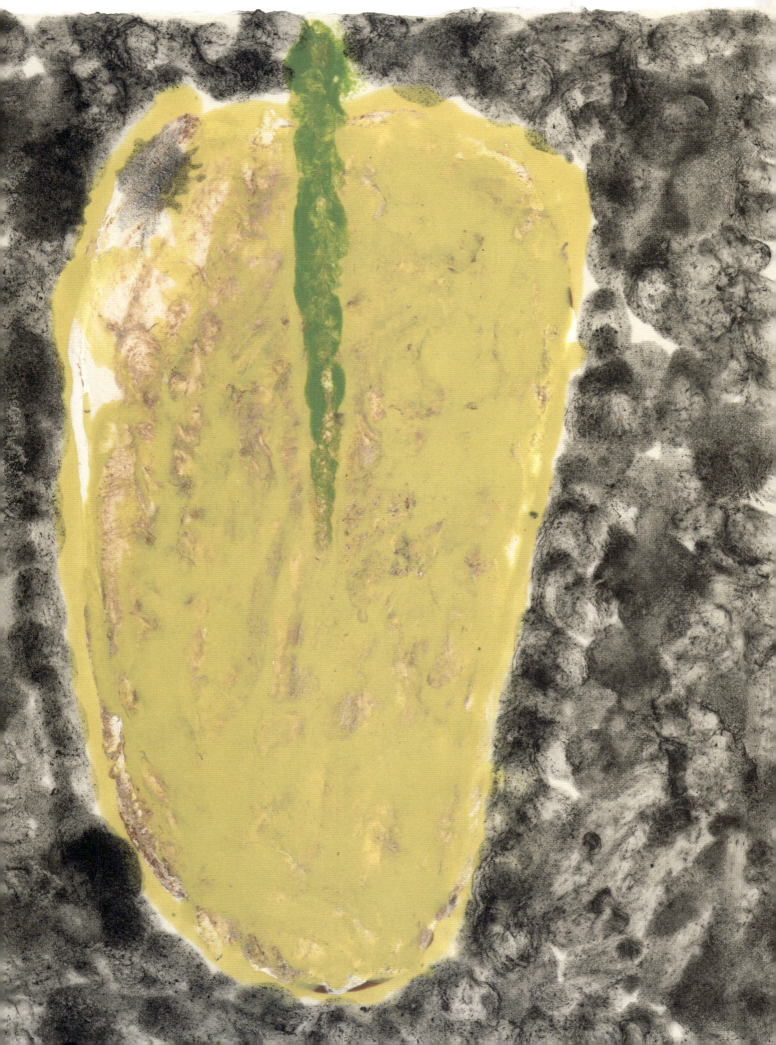

a Feathered mockingbird also called Fairgreen Drive home. It built its nest in a thick bush that grew outside the girl's window

In early spring the mockingbird laid green-blue eggs with brown spots. Both mockingbird parents guarded the eggs from curious fingers and hungry creatures

In the afternoons when the girl walked home from school the birds screeched, beat their wings wildly, and chased her with swooping dives she covered her head with her hands and made a run for the front door

Across the street from the pink house was a small park where the girl liked to play.
The park was home to a large Banyan tree that was only a seed when it arrived in Miami Beach.
The curious girl learned the seed traveled across the seas from the Island of Java, kept moist in damp blotting paper

The Banyan seed sprouted and grew quickly, happy to be alive

The girl would often climb the tree. In the beginning it wasn't easy to get a foothold to boost herself up to the first branch and find a place to sit. The tree trunk was wide, and the bark was smooth. She struggled

Then the girl reached out to grab a handful of long stringy roots that hung down from the tree's limbs. Now she could pull herself up. She felt like a little animal clinging to the roots in midair

Once she was up in the tree the world outside fell away.
Time seemed to stop.
She listened to the sweet sound of bird song, the first music.
She heard the invisible voice of the wind, felt the wings of insects moving air.
She thought about the connection between everything around her, like constellations in the sky.
She held on tight to the thick branch between her legs so she wouldn't fall while her head was spinning with thoughts she didn't quite understand.
She was certain she could even feel the earth revolving

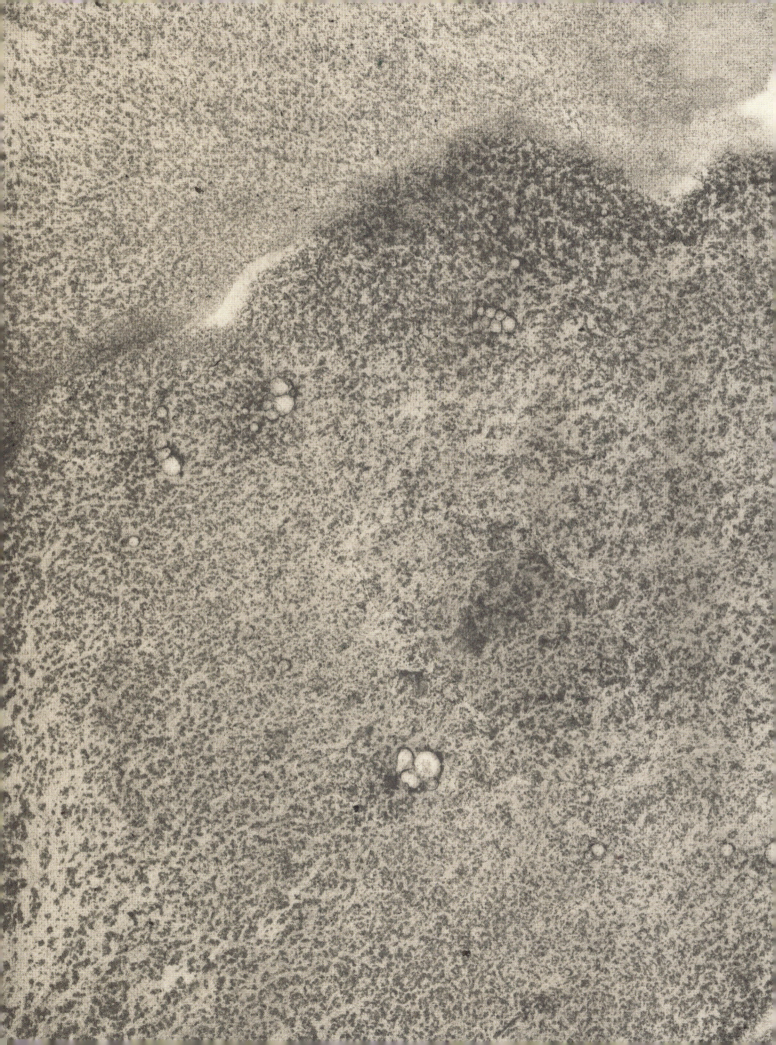

She could smell the aroma
of earth
as if it had just exhaled
its breath

She thought about
her life
and the life of the
Tree
How they both began
their existence as
tiny seeds

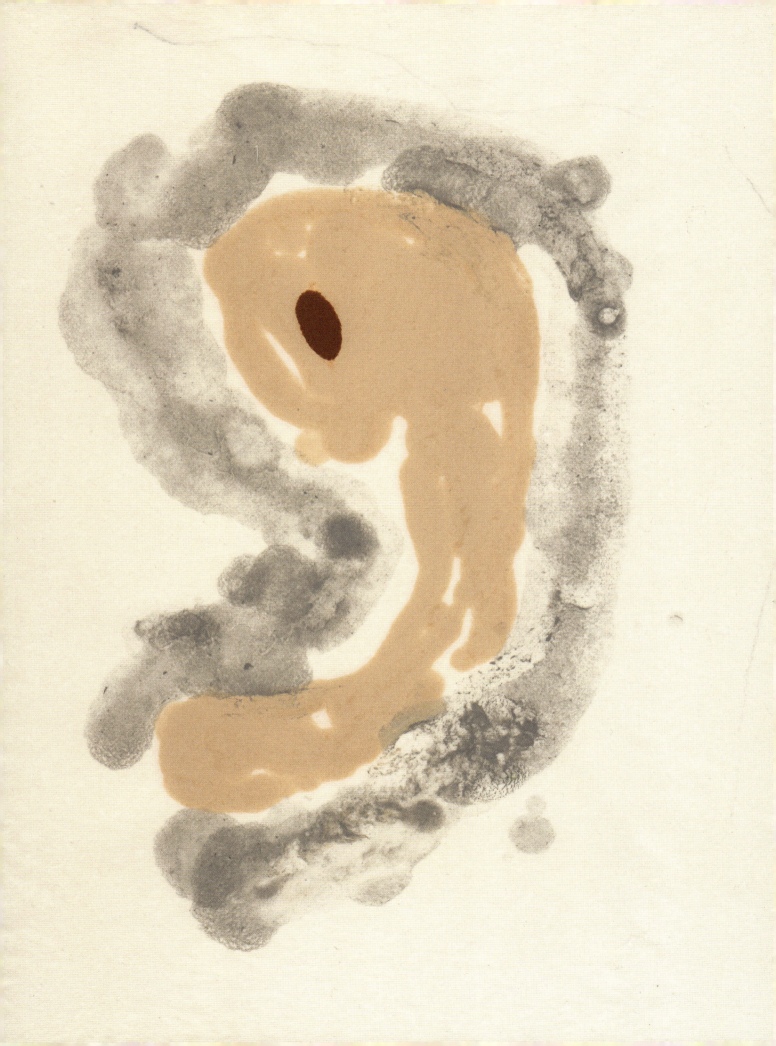

The dense leaves around her felt soft against her skin. The girl noticed the leaves had veins. She held up her hand: veins

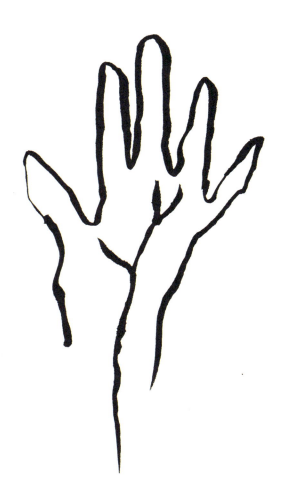

The heat of the day created moisture rising from the rich soil below, an accumulation of years and years of falling leaves decaying.

The girl's senses were pulsing, awake to the wonders of life in her hideaway. The Banyan Tree's majesty stirred her spirit

at night
in her bed
she dreamed
about the
tree.
It was as
if she had
come under
a spell

as time passed the girl watched the tree expand. The roots she clung to in order to climb had grown long and wide. They now reached the earth and dug past the ground cover of rotten leaves, into the soil, touching the limestone core below, the bone of miami Beach

Thousands of years ago
millions of tiny creatures
from an ancient sea,
shells and corals, had
formed this stone under
the tree, but the girl
couldn't see them.
She also could no longer
find the place she climbed
when she first discovered
the tree.
The Banyan had become a
small forest

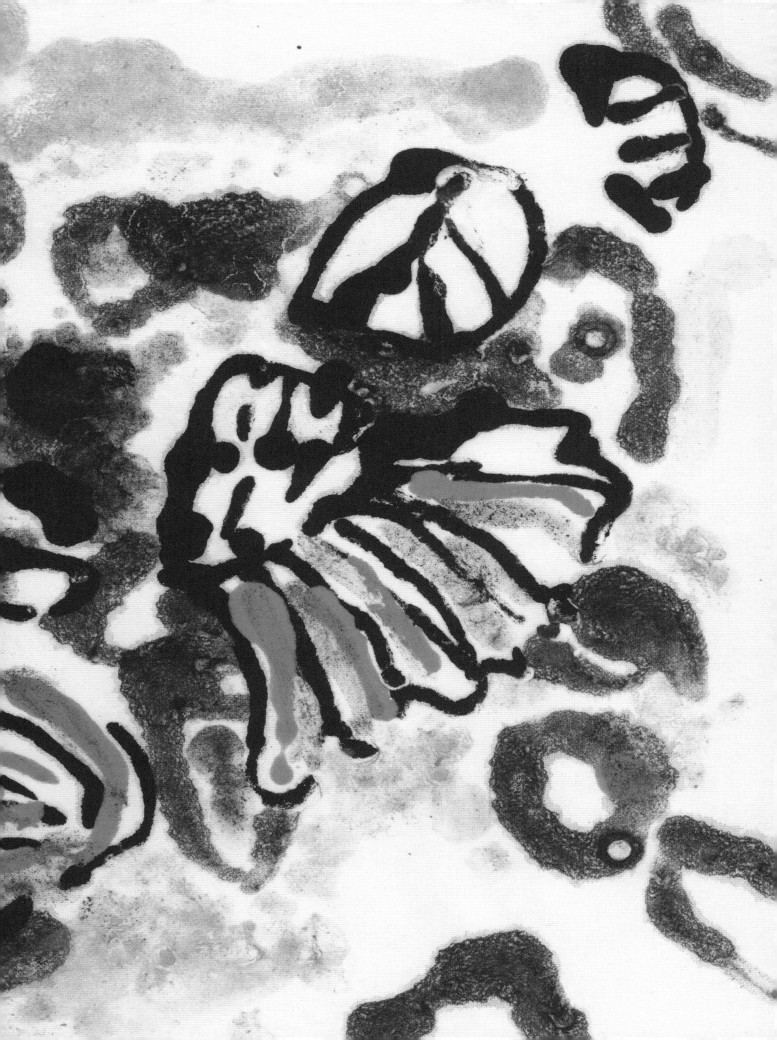

a pair of egrets arrived early mornings to find food in the long, wet grasses that now surrounded the Banyan tree

Wet grasses

While the tree was growing the girl was growing too. Childhood was behind her and she climbed less often. Now when she visited the tree her time was spent on the ground looking up at the dense green canopy. She liked the sound of the crunch of dry leaves beneath her feet as she walked around the tree's circumference. The deep shade offered her once again the sense of isolation she periodically craved, though she hadn't named it yet. She just enjoyed it.

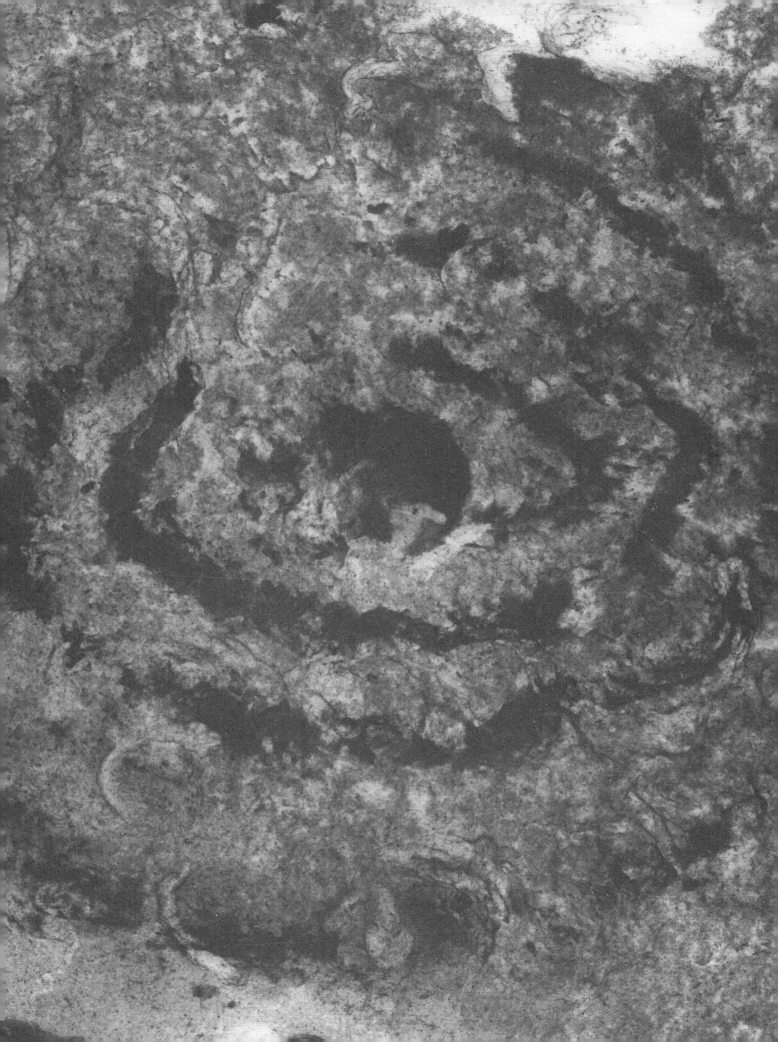

One day the girl was invited to a costume party. She decided to gather enough leaves from the Banyan Tree to cover her body and sew them together to make a dress.
She would pretend to be Eve.
The Banyan tree had always been her garden of Eden

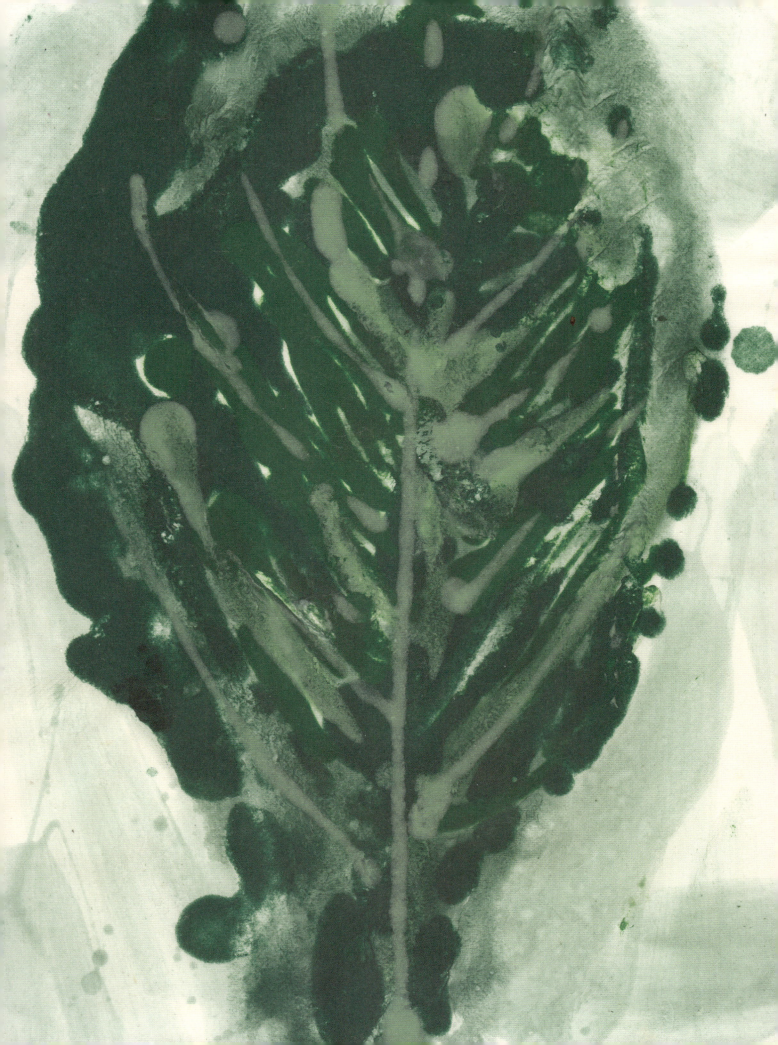

The morning of the party the girl crossed the street and picked fresh leaves early. She chose large ones, thick and shiny, still moist from morning dew. Carefully the girl carried her leaves home and laid them out on the bedroom floor in the shape of her body

She began to stitch, using green thread to hide her work. She wanted the dress to appear as if it was grown by the tree

When it was time for the party the girl lifted the dress up and tried to put it over her head. An unexpected thing happened. The weight of the leaves was too heavy for the thread. The leaves began to tear and fall downwards. The girl fought back tears and disappointment. Her idea wasn't working the way she imagined. She didn't want to miss the party. She sat on the floor to think about what to do next

the girl's mother had peeked into the girl's bedroom during the afternoon and watched her daughter working on her costume.
Now she entered the room, looked at the leaf dress, and had an idea.
She went to the girl's closet and took out a full slip

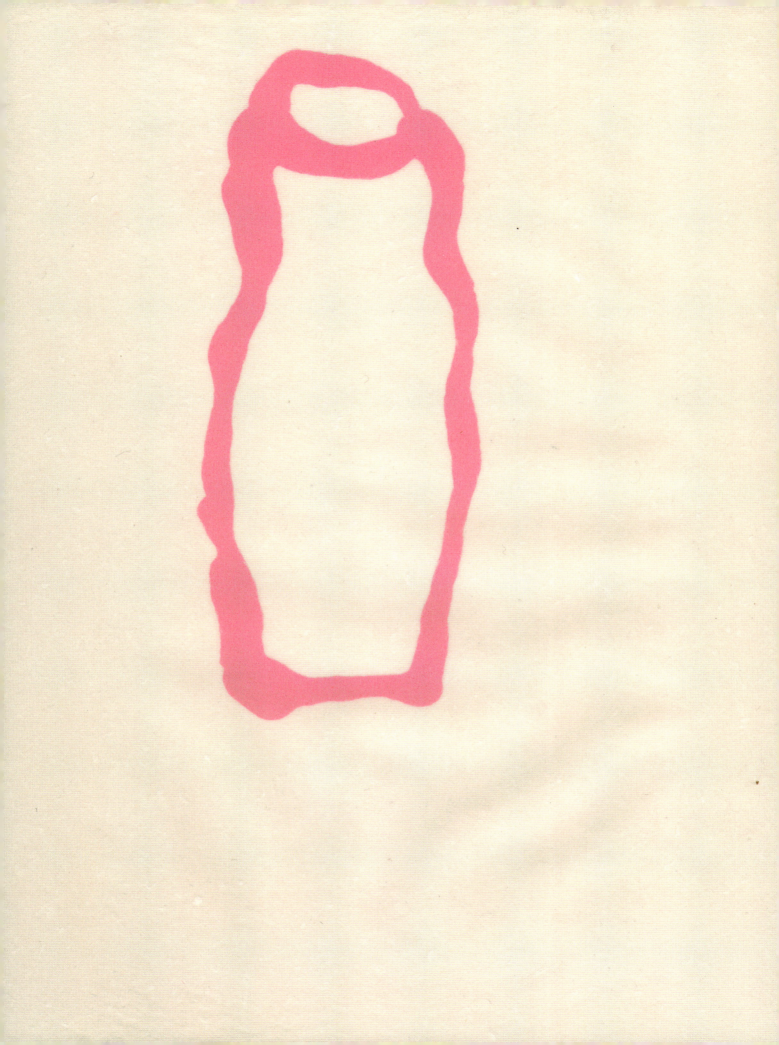

then she pushed the slip up between the front and back of the leaf dress and stitched the slip and dress together. Now the leaves had support
Then the mother lifted the slip over the girl's head and the leaves stayed in place
It was a beautiful dress and the girl smiled happily
She hugged her mother and went to the costume party as Eve

As the years went by the girl
grew up, left home just like
the mockingbirds
and like the mockingbirds
returned each year to
Fairgreen Drive
The street has remained
crooked

Though her home was
Far away
She brought her children
to climb the Banyan Tree
and experience its
wonders

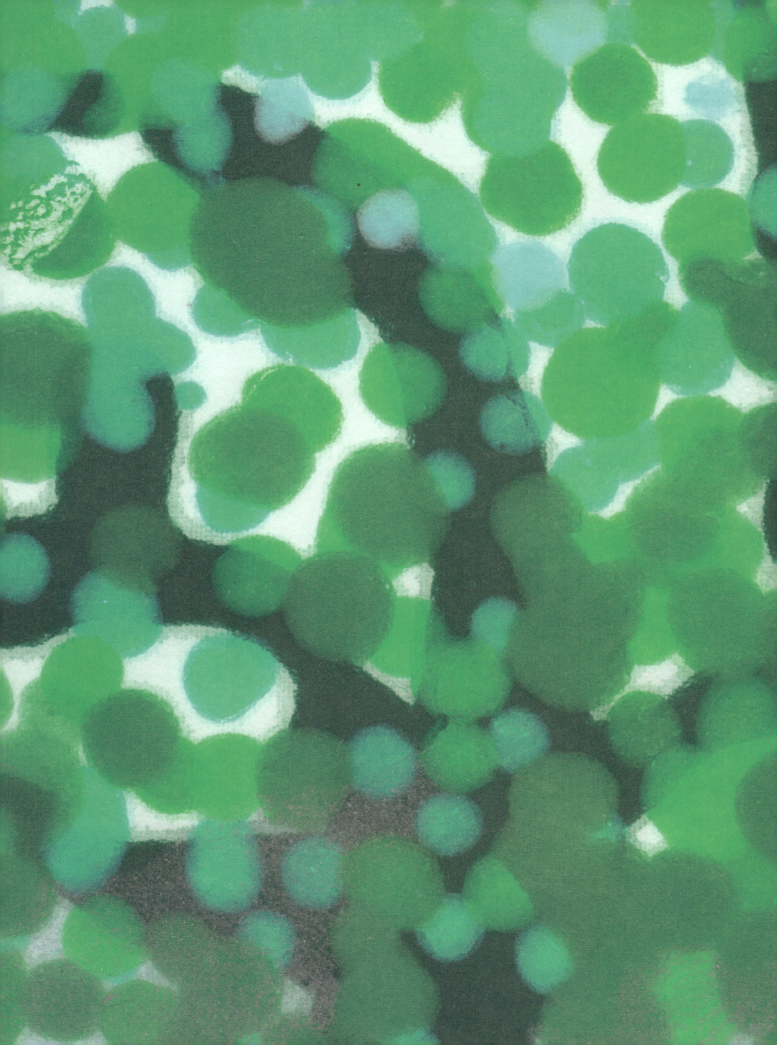

This book was inspired by Miami Beach Mayor Dan Gelber.

Michele Oka Doner's relationship from an early age with a banyan tree close to her home has been a source of inspiration for her six decades of work as a world-renowned artist and author. In 2022 the City of Miami Beach appointed her Guardian of the Great Miami Beach Banyan Tree and Ambassador of Arts and Culture.

Artist and Author
Michele Oka Doner

Art
Art by Michele Oka Doner created at
Dieu Donné, Brooklyn, New York
Assisted by Tatiana Ginsberg and Jordan Doner

Hand Lettering
Michele Oka Doner

Publisher & Creative Director
Ilona Oppenheim

Art Director & Designer
Jefferson Quintana

Printing
Printed and bound in China by
Shenzhen Reliance Printers

Cover and Back Cover
Art and hand lettering by
Michele Oka Doner

A Seed Takes Root: A True Story copyright © 2023 Michele Oka Doner

All rights reserved. No part of this publication may be reproduced or transmitted in any form or by any means, electronic or mechanical, including photocopy, recording, or any other information storage-and-retrieval system, without written permission from Tra Publishing.

ISBN: 979-8-9866406-4-8

A Seed Takes Root: A True Story is printed on Forest Stewardship Council certified paper from well-managed forests. The cover is derived from tree bark. Tra Publishing is committed to sustainability in its materials and practices.

Tra Publishing
245 NE 37th Street
Miami, FL 33137
trapublishing.com

[T] tra.publishing